CONTENTS

PAGES 4-5 **Characters and Icons** PAGES 6-7 **World Map**

PAGES 8-17

VOCABULARY
sit down, stand up, talk, clean up, shout, run
the alphabet

GRAMMAR
Don't shout.
Sit down, please.
How do you spell ...?

FEATURES
Country: Canada
World Music Song: The ABC Song
Phonics: ake, ate

PAGES 18-27

VOCABULARY
second, minute, hour, morning, afternoon, evening
get up, have breakfast, go to school, have lunch, have dinner, go to sleep

GRAMMAR
What time is it?
It's ... o'clock.
I ... at ... o'clock.

FEATURES
Country: Germany
World Music Song: My Busy Day
Phonics: ime, ine

PAGES 28-29 **Progress Check Units 1 & 2** PAGES 30-31 **Steam Challenge 1**

PAGES 32-41

VOCABULARY
sheep, chicken, donkey, duck, goat, cow
ladybug, grasshopper, caterpillar, mosquito, butterfly, ant

GRAMMAR
This is / That's a ...
These / Those are ...
What's this / that?
It's a / an ...
What are these / those?
They're ...

FEATURES
Country: Kenya
World Music Song: Itchy, Ouchy Mosquito
Phonics: one, ose

PAGES 42-51

VOCABULARY
peppers, carrots, potatoes, onions, beans, tomatoes
cookies, French fries, hamburgers, sandwiches, ice pops, pancakes

GRAMMAR
Do you like ...?
Yes, I do. / No, I don't.
I like ...
I don't like ...

FEATURES
Country: Turkey
World Music Song: I Like Food!
Phonics: une, oon

PAGES 52-53 **Progress Check Units 3 & 4** PAGES 54-55 **Steam Challenge 2**

PAGES 56-65

VOCABULARY
play the guitar, speak Vietnamese, climb a tree, touch your toes, do taekwondo, jump rope
fly, swim, hop, sing, walk, ride a horse

GRAMMAR
Can you ...?
Yes, I can. / No, I can't.
I / He / She / They can ...
I / He / She / They can't ...

FEATURES
Country: South Korea
World Music Song: I Can Do It!
Phonics: ea, ee

UNIT 6
PAGES 66-75

VOCABULARY
play soccer, watch TV, sing karaoke, play computer games, read books, play board games

draw, make models, listen to music, dance, paint, do puzzles

GRAMMAR
What do you like doing?
I like ...-ing.
I don't like ...-ing.
He / She likes ...-ing.
He / She doesn't like ...-ing.

FEATURES
Country: Argentina
World Music Song: Playing with Friends
Phonics: ai, ay

PAGES 76-77 **Progress Check Units 5 & 6**   PAGES 78-79 **Steam Challenge 3**

UNIT 7
PAGES 80-89

VOCABULARY
house, castle, boat, trailer, apartment, cave

ocean, desert, jungle, woods, city, country

GRAMMAR
He / She / It lives in ...
Where do you live?
I live in ...

FEATURES
Country: Mongolia
World Music Song: Where Do You Live?
Phonics: igh, y, ie

UNIT 8
PAGES 90-99

VOCABULARY
piano, trumpet, tambourine, violin, drums, recorder

Sunday, Monday, Tuesday, Wednesday, Thursday, Friday, Saturday

GRAMMAR
Do you play ...?
Yes, I do. / No, I don't.
Does he / she ... on ...?
Yes, he / she does.
No, he / she doesn't.

FEATURES
Country: Australia
World Music Song: Action Girl
Phonics: oa, ow

PAGES 100-101 **Progress Check Units 7 & 8**   PAGES 102-103 **Steam Challenge 4**

UNIT 9
PAGES 104-113

VOCABULARY
airplane, bus, helicopter, car, train, motorcycle

Multiples of ten: 10-100

GRAMMAR
I don't go to ... by ...
I go by ...
He / She doesn't go to ... by ...
He / She goes by ...

How many ... are there?
There are ...

FEATURES
Country: Thailand
World Music Song: The Picnic Box
Phonics: ue, ew

UNIT 10
PAGES 114-123

VOCABULARY
shirt, pants, skirt, shoes, sweater, sneakers

long, short, big, small, old, new

GRAMMAR
This is ...'s ...
These are ...'s ...
He / She has ...

FEATURES
Country: Peru
World Music Song: Our Clothes
Phonics: th

PAGES 124-125 **Progress Check Units 9 & 10**   PAGES 126-127 **Steam Challenge 5**

PAGE 128 # GRAMMAR GUIDE

3

CHARACTERS AND ICONS

"Hi! My name's Niki."

"I'm Bubba."

"We're explorers."

"Are you ready to learn English? Come on! Let's go!"

LOOK AND DO / LISTEN AND DO
Activities to interpret the picture of the unit opener pages

LISTEN
Audio tracks to practice listening skills

WORLD MUSIC
Songs with a World Music flavor

TEMPLATE
Photocopiable Language File activities to use in class

 BE sociable and creative. Know yourself!

 THINK critically when you use information!

 LEARN to do things by yourself. Learn how to learn!

 COLLABORATE / COMMUNICATE with others. Teamwork is cool!

 ACT respectfully, be tolerant, and friendly!

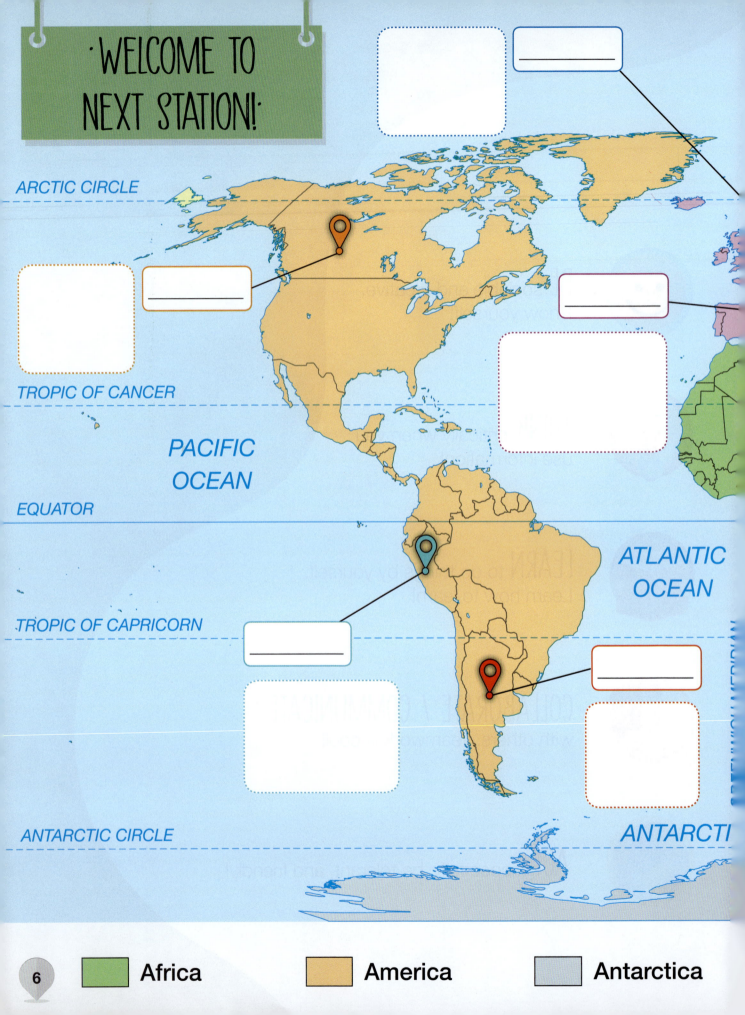

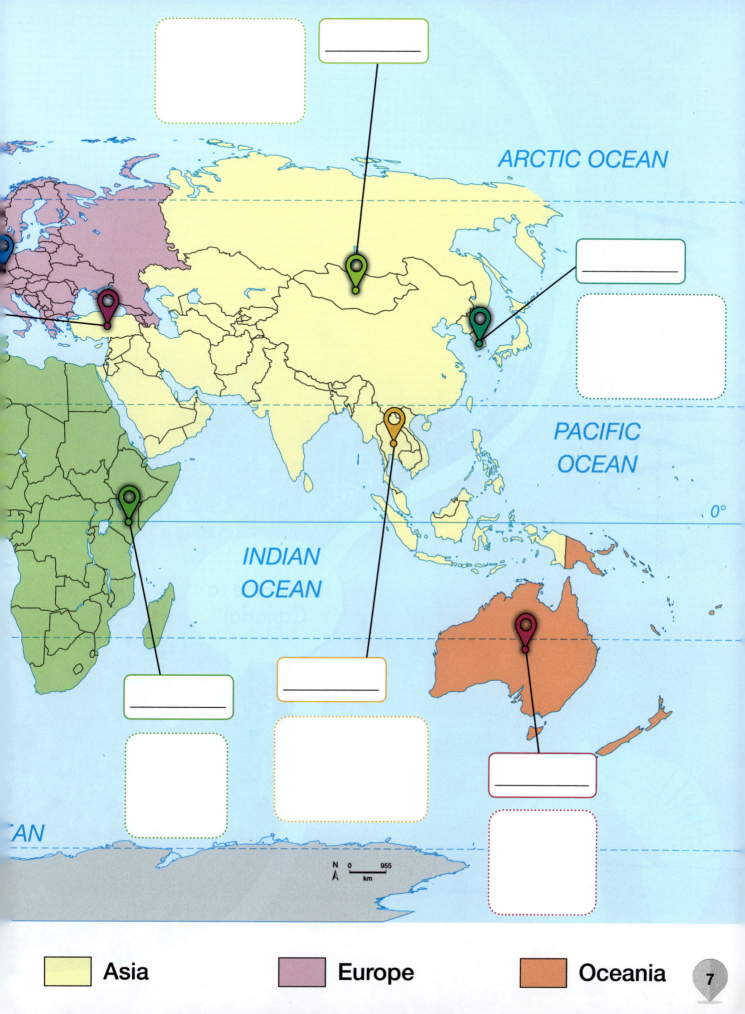

UNIT 1

Lesson 1

VOCABULARY

 TRACK 2

1 Listen, point, and say.

1 stand up

3 talk

2 sit down

4 clean up

5 shout

6 run

2 Look and circle.

1 shout / clean up

2 talk / run

3 stand up / sit down

3 Play the Action Game.

Sit down.

WORKBOOK page 4

10

Lesson 2

GRAMMAR

Don't shout.
Sit down, please.

 1 Listen, read, and say.

TRACK 3

 2 Number in order.

1 up, ◯   please. ◯   Clean ◯
2 down. ◯   Don't ◯   sit ◯

 3 Play the Please Game.

WORKBOOK page 5

GRAMMAR GUIDE page 129

Lesson 3

SOUNDS GREAT

 TRACK 4

1 Listen and chant.

Look at my cake!
It's a snake in a lake.
Take a plate!

 TRACK 5

2 Listen and say.

a k e   a t e

cake

plate

snake

lake

3 Look and write.

____ ____ ake

____ ____ ate

____ ake

____ ake

 4 Read the chant and underline *ake* and *ate*.

WORKBOOK
page 6

12

Lesson 4   ·READING TIME·

1 Listen and read.

2 Read the story again. Check (✓) the value.

Eat fruit. ◯   Be polite. ◯

3 Circle the polite words. Do you use these words?

please / don't / thank you / sorry / cherries

WORKBOOK
page 7

UNIT 1

Lesson 5

VOCABULARY

 TRACK 7

1 Listen, point, and sing. **The ABC Song**

1   A B C D E F G

2   H I J K L M N

3   O P Q R S T U V

4   W X Y Z

2 Ask and answer.

Yellow, 3.

Brown, 4.

S.

Y.

TEMPLATE 1

3 Complete. Then write the secret words.

14

WORKBOOK
page 8

Lesson 6

GRAMMAR

How do you spell "snake"?

 1 Listen, read, and say.

 2 Number in order.

do ◯   spell ◯   you ◯   How ◯   "dog"? ◯

 3 Ask and answer.

Lesson 7

· FUN READER ·

LET'S VISIT CANADA

1 Read about national favorites from Canada.

Hi, I'm Sara. My favorite sport is ice hockey. It's the national sport of Canada. Let's play, OK? Don't sit down! It's cold. Skate with me, please. It's fun!

This is a beaver. It's the national animal of Canada! Beavers are brown and have black eyes. They're cute! There are lots of beavers in Canada. Are there beavers in your country?

Think Twice

1 Circle.

Ice hockey / Soccer is the national sport of Canada.

The brown bear / beaver is the national animal of Canada.

2 What is the national sport of your country?

16

Lesson 8

SPEAKING TIME

1 Draw, write, and say.

> The national animal of Canada is a beaver. What's the national animal of your country?

NEW FRIENDS

1 Complete the conversation. Choose your response.

> Hi! I'm Sara. What's your name?

> My name's _____.

> How do you spell your name?

> _____.

2 Act out the conversation.

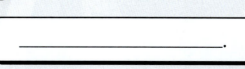

GERMANY

ARRIVAL ← GERMANY 18 AUG BERLIN AIRPORT

Welcome to Germany!

UNIT 2

Lesson **1**

VOCABULARY

 1 Listen, point, and say.

1 second

2 minute

3 hour

4 morning

5 afternoon

6 evening

 2 Listen and circle.

1 15 minutes / 15 seconds

2 7 minutes / 7 hours

3 5 seconds / 5 hours

 3 Look, write, and act.

1 Good _____

2 Good _____

3 Good _____

WORKBOOK
page 11

20

Lesson 2

GRAMMAR

What time is it?
It's eight **o'clock**.

TRACK 12

1 Listen, read, and say.

TRACK 13

2 Listen, draw, and write.

1 What _____?

It's _____.

2 What _____ is it?

_____.

 3 Make a clock. Ask and answer.

TEMPLATE 2

WORKBOOK page 12

GRAMMAR GUIDE page 129

Lesson 3

SOUNDS GREAT

TRACK 14

1 Listen and chant.

Nine dimes in a line.
Look! One more dime.
One more time!

TRACK 15

2 Listen and say.

time   dime   nine   line

3 Look and write the letters in order.

   9

neil   tmie   ienn   eidm

_____   _____   _____   _____

4 Read the chant and underline *ime* and *ine*.

WORKBOOK
page 13

22

Lesson 4

·READING TIME·

🔊 **TRACK 16** **1** Listen and read.

⭐ 2 Read the story again. Check (✓) the **value** ⭐.

Look at the time. ◯   Don't be late. ◯

😊 3 How do you feel when you are late? Circle.

WORKBOOK page 14

23

Lesson 5

VOCABULARY

1 Listen, point, and say.

1 get up

2 have breakfast

3 go to school

4 have lunch

5 have dinner

6 go to sleep

2 Listen and say what's next.

3 Sing and act. **My Busy Day**

I get up and I have breakfast,
At the start of every day.
I go to school and I have lunch,
I work and then I play.
I have dinner with my family.
Then I have time to play.
I go to bed and I go to sleep.
It's a busy, busy, day!

WORKBOOK page 15

24

Lesson 6

GRAMMAR

I get up **at** seven **o'clock**.

1 Listen, read, and say.

2 Complete about you.

1 I have breakfast at _____ o'clock.

2 _____ go to school at _____.

3 _____ have dinner at _____.

3 Play the Mime Game.

WORKBOOK page 16

GRAMMAR GUIDE page 129

Lesson 7

· FUN READER ·

LET'S VISIT GERMANY

1 Read about traditional food from Germany.

Hello! I'm Gunther. I'm from Hanover, in Germany.

Look at this! It's a traditional German chocolate cake! It's called Black Forest cake. It has chocolate, cream, and cherries. It's delicious. I eat chocolate cake in the afternoon and evening! Is it time for cake?

Think Twice

1 Read and check (✓).

Black Forest cake has chocolate, ◯

cream, ◯ trees, ◯

cherries, ◯ pears. ◯

2 When do you eat cake?

26

Lesson 8 · SPEAKING TIME ·

  1 Draw, write, and say.

Mmm! Traditional chocolate cake from Germany … _____ is a traditional dessert from my country.

1 Complete the conversation. Choose your response.

Would you like to try some Black Forest cake?

Yes, please. ○
No, thanks. ○

2 Act out the conversation.

PROGRESS CHECK

✓ **1** Read, look, and write the numbers.

1 Clean up, please.   **2** Sit down, please.   **3** Don't talk.   **4** Don't run.

✓ **2** Look, say, and write.

_____

_____

_____

_____

THINK AGAIN!

An animal from Canada is the _____.

My favorite lesson is on page _____.

The national sport of Canada is _____.

28 | WORKBOOK page 18 | STICKERS | PASSPORT page 2

PROGRESS CHECK

✓ **1** Read and draw.

 **1** It's three o'clock.

 **2** It's eight o'clock.

✓ **2** Look and write.

 1 It's _____.

 2 It's _____.

✓ **3** Look and complete.

❶ I _____ at eight o'clock.

❷ I _____ at twelve o'clock.

❸ I _____ at seven o'clock.

❹ I _____ at eight o'clock.

THINK AGAIN!

A famous food in Germany is _____.

My favorite picture is on page _____.

A traditional object from Germany is _____.

WORKBOOK page 19 STICKERS PASSPORT page 4

29

CANADA

The Peace Tower clock in Ottawa, Canada.

Mythical figures adorn the building.

Gargoyles are decorative and help keep rain water away.

STEAM

TEAM NAME

Why do we need to know the time?

1 Get materials.

play dough

toothpicks

Super Star Challenge

ruler

scissors

colored pencils

glue stick

paper

A clock tower has one or more clock faces.

The Peace Tower clock was a gift from the UK in 1927.

The clock of the New Town Hall was first heard in 1908.

30

CHALLENGE 1 · BUILD A CLOCK TOWER ·

GERMANY

② Look at the geometric shapes below. Draw your plan.

square

cube

triangle

tetrahedron

③ Build a clock tower.

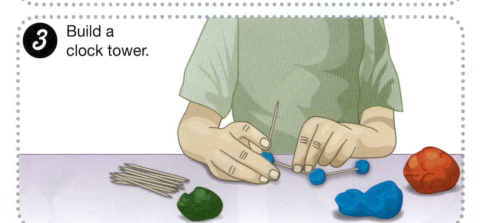

The clock tower of the New Town Hall in Munich, Germany.

The Glockenspiel, a tourist attraction at the New Town Hall.

④ Name your clock tower.
_____

⑤ How tall is it?
_____ cm

Super Star Challenge
Add a flag, clock, gargoyles, and figures to your tower.

Did your clock tower match your drawing? Why or why not?

Some of the 32 figures on the Glockenspiel stage.

TEAMWORK ★★★★★

31

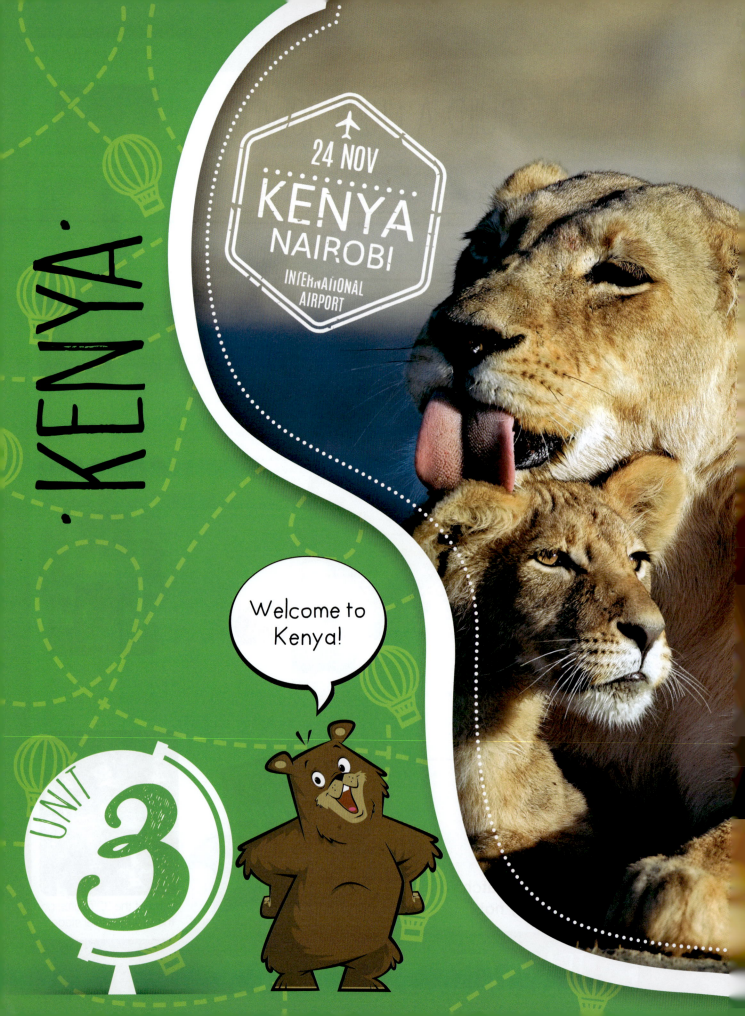

Lesson 1

VOCABULARY

TRACK 21

1 Listen, point, and say.

1 duck
2 goat
3 donkey
4 cow
5 sheep
6 chicken

TRACK 22

2 Listen and guess.

3 Look and complete.

1 It's a _____.

2 It's a _____.

3 It's a _____.

4 It's a _____.

34

WORKBOOK page 20

Lesson 2

 1 Listen, read, and say.

GRAMMAR

This is a duck.
That's a cow.
These are goats.
Those are chickens.

2 Look and circle.

1 **This is** / **That's** a bird.   **2** **These** / **Those** are chickens.

 3 Draw and talk about your animals.

WORKBOOK page 21

GRAMMAR GUIDE page 130

35

Lesson 3

SOUNDS GREAT

TRACK 24

1 Listen and chant.

The bone is under a stone but his nose is in a rose!

TRACK 25

2 Listen and say.

bone   stone   nose   rose

3 Connect and write.

1 s   t   o   n   e _____

2 n   o   s   e   _____

3 r   o   s   e   _____

4 b   o   n   e   _____

4 Read the chant and underline *one* and *ose*.

WORKBOOK page 22

36

Lesson 4   ·READING TIME·

TRACK 26

1 Listen and read.

 2 Read the story again. Check (✓) the value.

Be responsible. ◯   Listen to your grandma. ◯

 3 What responsible things do you do? Circle.

37

Lesson 5

VOCABULARY

TRACK 27

1 Listen, point, and say.

1 ladybug

2 grasshopper

3 caterpillar

4 mosquito

5 butterfly

6 ant

 2 Look and write.

1 These are _____.

2 This is a _____.

3 _____.

4 _____.

WORKBOOK page 24

38

Lesson 6

TRACK 28

1 Listen, read, and say.

GRAMMAR

What's this / that?
It's a caterpillar / **an** ant.
What are these / those?
They're grasshoppers.

- What's that?
- It's a caterpillar.
- What are those?
- They're mosquitoes. Watch out!

TRACK 29

2 Sing. **Itchy, Ouchy Mosquito**

What are these? What are these?
They're green grasshoppers.
What are those? What are those?
They're curly caterpillars.

What's that? What's that?
It's a shiny black cat.
And what's this? Ooh! Ouch! Stop! Oh, no!
It's an itchy, ouchy, itchy, ouchy mosquito!

WORKBOOK page 25

GRAMMAR GUIDE page 130

UNIT 3 · Lesson 7

· FUN READER ·

LET'S VISIT KENYA

1 Read about animals in Kenya.

Hi! My name's Zalika. I'm from Kenya.

Kenya is famous for its animals. There are many different animals there. These are zebras. They're black and white. They are very similar to donkeys and horses.

What are these? They're birds! Pink birds! And they are called pink flamingos.
They are very, very beautiful!

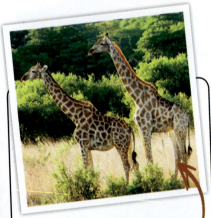

Look at those giraffes! Wow! Their necks are long! Giraffes eat green leaves from trees for breakfast, lunch, and dinner! They love leaves.

Think Twice

1 Read and write *z* (zebra), *g* (giraffe), or *f* (flamingo).

It's a bird. ◯   It's black and white. ◯

It has a long neck. ◯

2 Are there pink flamingos in your country?

Lesson 8

·SPEAKING TIME·

 1 Draw, write, and say.

This is a giraffe from Kenya.

This is a / an _____ from my country.

1 Complete the conversation.

Hi. We have a lot of giraffes in my country. I like giraffes.

I like giraffes, too.

I prefer _____.

2 Act out the conversation.

41

Lesson 1

· VOCABULARY ·

TRACK 30

1 Listen, point, and say.

1 peppers

2 potatoes

3 onions

4 carrots

5 beans

6 tomatoes

 2 Count and write.

1 There are three peppers.
2 _____.
3 _____.
4 _____.
5 _____.
6 _____.

 3 Ask and answer.

How many peppers are there?

There are three.

44

WORKBOOK
page 27

Lesson 2

TRACK 31

1 Listen, read, and say.

GRAMMAR

Do you like carrots?
Yes, **I do**. / No, **I don't**.

2 Complete and color your answer.

			Yes, I do.	No, I don't.
1	_Do you like_ onions?	○	○
2	_____ peppers?	○	○
3	_____ beans?	○	○
4	_____ potatoes?	○	○
5	_____ tomatoes?	○	○

3 Ask and answer.

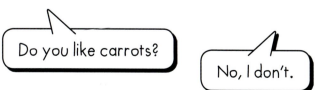

45

Lesson 3

SOUNDS GREAT

 TRACK 32

1 Listen and chant.

The boy plays a tune,
Under the moon.
And the girl eats prunes
With her spoon.

 TRACK 33

2 Listen, say, and color.

 une  oon

spoon

prune

moon

tune

3 Write and match.

oon   une

sp ___ ___   t ___ ___ ___   m ___ ___ ___   pr ___ ___ ___

4 Read the chant and underline *une* and *oon*.

WORKBOOK page 29

46

Lesson 4   · READING TIME ·

 TRACK 34

1 Listen and read.

 2 Read the story again. Check (✓) the value ⭐.

Say "Thank you." ◯   Try new things. ◯

 3 Look at the story and answer.

Do you try new things when you eat outside your house?

Do you like to try things that look unusual?

WORKBOOK
page 30

47

Lesson 5

VOCABULARY

TRACK 35

1 Listen, point, and say.

1. hamburgers
2. pancakes
3. sandwiches
4. French fries
5. cookies
6. ice pops

2 Match.

ice pops
French fries
sandwiches
pancakes
hamburgers
cookies

TEMPLATE 4

3 Write. Then ask and answer.

How do you spell "hamburgers"?

H-a-m-b-u-r-g-e-r-s.

WORKBOOK page 31

48

Lesson 6

1 Listen, read, and say.

GRAMMAR
I like hamburgers.
I don't like peppers.

2 Talk to a friend.

beans   carrots   cookies
French fries   hamburgers   ice pops
onions   pancakes   peppers

I like ice pops.
I don't like onions.

3 Sing. **I Like Food!**

Do you like hamburgers?
Yes, I do. Yes, I do.
I like hamburgers with onions.

Do you like bananas?
Yes, I do. Yes, I do.
I like bananas with hot pancakes.

Do you like everything?
No, I don't. No, I don't.
I don't like spiders and I don't like snakes!

WORKBOOK page 32

GRAMMAR GUIDE page 130

Lesson 7

· FUN READER ·

LET'S VISIT TURKEY

1 Read about food markets in Turkey.

Hello, I'm Ahmet, and this is my dad.

Look at his vegetable stand. There are peppers, beans, and tomatoes.

This is a traditional market in Turkey. There are many different foods here. And they are all fresh and delicious. Don't forget, eat lots of fresh vegetables!

This is a famous candy from Turkey. It's called Turkish delight. It's very sweet! And look at all the colors! Turkish delight is yellow, orange, or green!

Think Twice

1. What can you buy at the market? Circle.

   cookies / beans / French fries / peppers / ice pops / tomatoes

2. Is there a similar type of food market in your town?

50

Lesson 8

SPEAKING TIME

 1 Draw, write, and say.

Turkish delight is a famous candy from Turkey. What candy is famous in your country?

_____ is a famous candy from my country.

NEW FRIENDS

1 Complete the conversation. Choose your response.

Do you like candy?

_____.

I have Turkish delight. Here, try one.

Thank you! ◯

No, thanks. ◯

2 Act out the conversation.

WORKBOOK page 33

51

UNIT 3

PROGRESS CHECK

✓ **1** Look, read, and number.

That's a monkey. **1**   Those are elephants. ◯   This is a ladybug. ◯

These are snakes. ◯   That's a butterfly. ◯   These are caterpillars. ◯

✓ **2** Look and write.

~~What's this?~~   What's that?   What are these?   What are those?

1 What's this? _____ It's a ladybug.

2 _____ They're caterpillars.

3 _____ They're elephants.

4 _____ It's a monkey.

THINK AGAIN!

Two animals from Kenya are _____ and _____.

My favorite lesson is on page _____.

Giraffes love to eat _____.

52

UNIT 4

PROGRESS CHECK

✓ **1** Complete and answer *Yes, I do.* or *No, I don't.*

1 Do you like _____? _____.

2 Do you like _____? _____.

3 Do you like _____? _____.

4 Do you like _____? _____.

5 Do you like _____? _____.

✓ **2** Look and write.

Niki — I like …
Bubba — I don't like …

1 I like tomatoes. | I don't like onions.

2 _____ | _____

3 _____ | _____

THINK AGAIN!

Two types of food from Turkey are _____ and _____.

My favorite picture is on page _____.

A traditional object from Turkey is _____.

WORKBOOK page 35   STICKERS   PASSPORT page 8

53

KENYA

The arid region below Mount Kenya.

Samburo child in traditional clothing.

Camel in the Chalbi desert, Kenya.

TEAM NAME

How many minutes does it take a camel to drink 113 liters of water? 13, 23, or 30?

1 Get materials.

paper squares

measuring cup with water

Dromedary camels have only one hump. The hump is full of fat.

Bactrian camels have two humps.

Camels can go 6 months without food or water. Their habitat is hot, dry, and sandy.

CHALLENGE 2

DESIGN A PAPER CUP

TURKEY

2 Design a paper cup. Follow the model.

1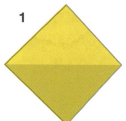
2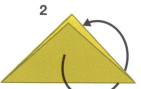
3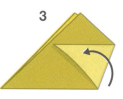
4
5
6
7

3 Fill it with water. Test your cup for 10 seconds.

Super Star Challenge: Design a cup using a different shape of paper that can hold water.

How do you conserve water?

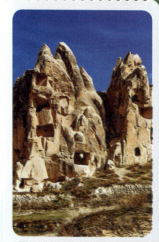
The semi-arid region of Cappadocia, in Turkey.

Turkish dancer in traditional clothing.

Camel with a child in Antalya, Turkey.

TEAMWORK

Lesson 1

TRACK 39

 1 Listen, point, and say.

2 Match and say.

do	rope
play	your toes
speak	the guitar
climb	a tree
touch	Vietnamese
jump	taekwondo

 3 Play the Whisper Game.

WORKBOOK page 36

58

Lesson 2

1 Listen, read, and say.

GRAMMAR
Can you play the guitar?
Yes, **I can**. / No, **I can't**.

 2 Write.

1 Can you speak English? _____.
2 Can you climb a tree? _____.
3 Can you do taekwondo? _____.
4 Can you play the guitar? _____.
5 Can you jump rope? _____.

 3 Ask and answer.

Can you speak Vietnamese?   No, I can't.

Lesson 3

SOUNDS GREAT

 TRACK 41

1 Listen and chant.

The teacher is under
A big, green tree.
"This is a bean.
Repeat after me!"

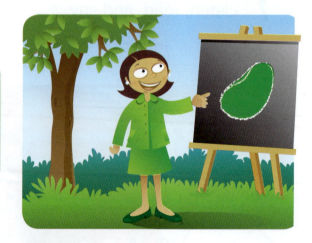

 TRACK 42

2 Listen, say, and color.

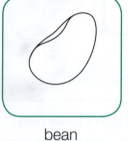      

green   bean   teacher   tree

 3 Write and match.

t ___ ___ cher   gr ___ ___ n   b ___ ___ n   tr ___ ___

 4 Read the chant and underline *ea* and *ee*.

WORKBOOK
page 38

Lesson 4 ·READING TIME·

1 Listen and read.

 2 Read the story again. Check (✓) the **value**.

Play music. ◯   Be positive. ◯

 3 What do you say when you are being positive?

No, I can't. ◯   Yes, I can. ◯

61

Lesson 5

VOCABULARY

TRACK 44

1 Listen, point, and say.

1 fly

2 swim

3 hop

4 sing

5 walk

6 ride a horse

2 Read and circle.

1 Can you swim?   Yes, I can. / No, I can't.
2 Can you hop?   Yes, I can. / No, I can't.
3 Can you walk?   Yes, I can. / No, I can't.
4 Can you fly?   Yes, I can. / No, I can't.
5 Can you ride a horse? Yes, I can. / No, I can't.
6 Can you sing?   Yes, I can. / No, I can't.

TEMPLATE 5

3 Complete the quiz. Ask and answer.

Can you swim?

Yes, I can.

WORKBOOK page 40

62

Lesson 6

 TRACK 45

1 Listen, read, and say.

GRAMMAR
I / He / She / They **can** sing.
I / He / She / They **can't** swim.

Bubba can sing and the birds can sing. I can't sing, but I can play the guitar.

 TRACK 46

2 Sing and act. **I Can Do It!**

I can speak Vietnamese,
I can do taekwondo.
I can swim, I can hop,
I can touch my big toe.

I can play the guitar,
I can jump up high.
But I can't, no, I can't,
I just can't fly!

WORKBOOK page 41

GRAMMAR GUIDE page 131

63

Lesson 7

FUN READER

LET'S VISIT SOUTH KOREA

1 Read about special events in South Korea.

Hi, I'm Jin. I'm from South Korea.

There are lots of festivals in South Korea. At the Moon Festival, some people play traditional games and eat special foods! People eat rice with nuts and beans. Do you like beans?

Dano is a Korean holiday. People sing traditional songs. They play drums and trumpets. They dance and play traditional games. And they wrestle! Can you wrestle?

Think Twice

1 Read and circle.

People eat special food at the Moon Festival. **True / False**

People play guitars on the Dano holiday. **True / False**

2 Can you name a special event in your country?

Lesson 8

SPEAKING TIME

1 Draw, write, and say.

At festivals in my country, people eat / play
_____.

NEW FRIENDS

1 Complete the conversation. Choose your response.

I can do taekwondo. Can you?

This is my sister. She can ride a horse. Can you?

Yes, I can. ◯
No, I can't, but I can _____. ◯

Yes, I can. ◯
No, I can't. ◯

2 Act out the conversation.

WORKBOOK page 42

65

Lesson 1

VOCABULARY

 1 Listen, point, and say.

1 play soccer

2 watch TV

3 sing karaoke

4 play computer games

5 read books

6 play board games

 2 Listen and guess.

 3 Check (✓) the activities in the pictures.

1 sing karaoke

2 play soccer

3 watch TV

4 play board games

5 read books

6 play computer games

68   WORKBOOK page 43

Lesson 2

1 Listen, read, and say.

GRAMMAR

What do you like doing?
I like read**ing**.
I don't like sing**ing**.

2 Look and complete.

- 😟 I ____don't like____ watching TV.
- 🙂 I _____ playing board games.
- 🙂 I _____ reading books.
- 😟 I _____ singing karaoke.

 3 Number in order. Ask and answer.

you ◯ What ① do ◯ doing? ◯ like ◯

I like playing board games.

Lesson 3

SOUNDS GREAT

TRACK 50

1 Listen and chant.

It's rainy today.
Let's play a game.
Sit down with me.
Let's make a train!

TRACK 51

2 Listen, say, and color.

rainy

play

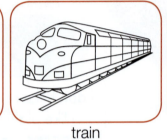
train

today

3 Look and write.

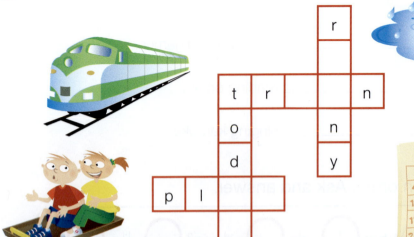

4 Read the chant and underline *ai* and *ay*.

70

WORKBOOK page 45

Lesson 4

· READING TIME ·

TRACK 52

1 Listen and read.

2 Read the story again. Check (✓) the *value*.

Value your friends. ◯   Play outdoors. ◯

3 What do you like doing with your friends?

reading ◯   playing soccer ◯   playing games ◯   watching TV ◯

WORKBOOK
page 46

Lesson 5

· VOCABULARY ·

TRACK 53

1 Listen, point, and say.

TRACK 54

2 Listen and write their names.

TEMPLATE 6

3 Complete, write, and say.

I like playing soccer and I like listening to music.

WORKBOOK page 47

Lesson

1 Listen, read, and say.

GRAMMAR
He / She likes reading.
He / She doesn't like singing.

2 Look and circle.

1 Bubba doesn't like singing.   True / False

2 Niki likes listening to music.   True / False

3 Sing and act. **Playing with Friends**

He likes reading books at school.
She likes swimming in the pool.

*But they both like playing with friends.
They both like playing with friends.*

She doesn't like climbing a tree.
He doesn't like watching TV.

Chorus

73

Lesson 7 — FUN READER

LET'S VISIT ARGENTINA

1 Read about a family from Argentina.

Hello! I'm Laura. I'm nine years old, and I'm from Buenos Aires, in Argentina.

I like playing soccer. Soccer is very popular in Argentina. We love playing soccer and watching it on TV.

This is my grandmother and grandfather. My grandma's name is Flora, and my grandpa's name is Miguel. My grandma doesn't like playing soccer! But she likes listening to music, and she likes dancing the tango. It's her favorite dance.

Think Twice

1 Circle.

   Flora likes playing soccer / listening to music / dancing.

2 Do you like dancing?

Lesson 8

SPEAKING TIME

1 Draw, write, and say.

People in Argentina like dancing.
People in my country like
_____.

NEW FRIENDS

1 Complete the conversation. Choose your response.

Hi. I like playing soccer.

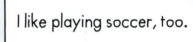

I like playing soccer, too. ◯

I don't like playing soccer. I like _____. ◯

2 Act out the conversation.

WORKBOOK
page 49

75

PROGRESS CHECK

✓ **1** Look and write. Ask and answer.

Can he _____?

_____.

Can he _____?

_____.

Can she _____?

_____.

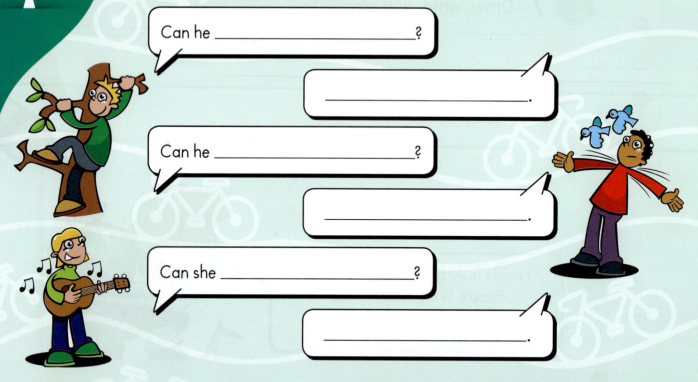

✓ **2** Write *can* or *can't*.

1 Dogs _____ do taekwondo.
2 Ducks _____ swim.
3 Donkeys _____ play the guitar.
4 Snakes _____ fly.
5 Grasshoppers _____ hop.
6 Cats _____ climb trees.

THINK AGAIN!

People eat _____ and _____ in South Korea.
My favorite lesson is on page _____.
A musical instrument popular in South Korea is _____.

UNIT 6 · PROGRESS CHECK ·

✓ **1** Look and write.

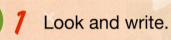
I like playing board games.

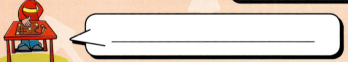

✓ **2** Match.

He likes   She likes   She likes

He likes   She likes   He likes

listening to music.

watching TV.

drawing.

making models.

painting.

reading books.

THINK AGAIN!

A dance from Argentina is _____.

My favorite picture is on page _____.

A popular activity in Argentina is _____.

WORKBOOK page 51   **STICKERS**   **PASSPORT** page 12

77

SOUTH KOREA

Janggu, a traditional Korean drum.

The *janggu* drum in a performance by a South Korean group.

Folk dancers with a *sogo* drum.

STEAM

TEAM NAME

What is sound? How does it travel?

1 Get materials.

cardboard

scissors

2 pieces of string

wooden stick

4 beads

markers

tape

2 Draw a cardboard circle. Cut it out.

A drum is a percussion instrument. It makes sound when hit. Drums can be very different in size and shape.

Korean CheonGo drum

djembe drum

spinning drum

78

CHALLENGE 3 · MAKE A SPINNING DRUM·

3 Ask an adult to make 2 small holes.

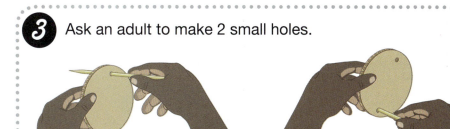

4 Add strings and beads.

5 Insert the stick into the cardboard circle and decorate.

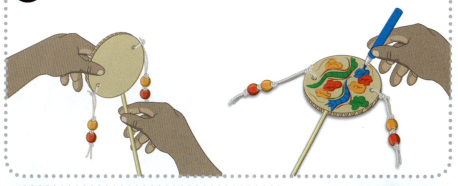

6 Test your drum.

What kind of drum is traditional in your culture? How is it played?

Super Star Challenge — Play in a drum parade.

ARGENTINA

Bombo legüero, a traditional drum from Argentina.

The *bombo legüero* in an opening festival in Argentina.

A folk dance accompanied by *bombo legüero*.

TEAMWORK ★★☆☆☆

Which animal doesn't live in Mongolia? Check (✓).

1 2 3 4

Lesson 1

· VOCABULARY ·

TRACK 57

1 Listen, point, and say.

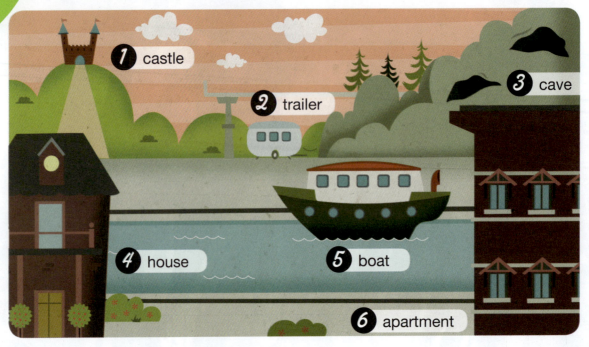

TRACK 58

2 Listen and say what's missing.

3 Draw your home and write.

This is _____.

82

WORKBOOK
page 52

Lesson 2

GRAMMAR

He / She / It lives in a house.

TRACK 59

1 Listen, read, and say.

 2 Play the Card Game.

83

Lesson 3

SOUNDS GREAT

 TRACK 60

1 Listen and chant.

The birds fly high in the sky.
The birds love apple pie.

 TRACK 61

2 Listen, say, and color.

pie   sky   fly   high

3 Write and match.

p ___ ___   h ___ ___ ___   sk ___   fl ___

 4 Read the chant and underline *igh, y,* and *ie.*

WORKBOOK page 54

84

Lesson 4 ·READING TIME·

TRACK 62

1 Listen and read.

 2 Read the story again. Check (✓) the value ⭐.

Welcome people. ◯   Talk to your neighbors. ◯

 3 What do you say to a new boy or girl in your class? Circle.

Come and play with us. / Do you like spiders?

WORKBOOK
page 55

85

Lesson 5

·VOCABULARY·

TRACK 63

1 Listen, point, and say.

1 ocean   **2** desert   **3** jungle

4 woods   **5** city   **6** country

2 Find and circle.

n	w	e	l	t	q	i	f	c	s	a	o	l	n	w
c	o	u	n	t	r	y	g	i	n	e	c	v	p	i
a	o	z	c	y	m	c	s	t	g	k	e	i	j	o
f	d	e	s	e	r	t	b	y	c	f	a	u	m	p
m	s	p	d	m	s	e	l	h	j	u	n	g	l	e

3 Complete.

1 The iguana lives in the _____.

2 The bird lives in the _____.

3 The bear lives in the _____.

4 The fish lives in the _____.

5 The cow lives in the _____.

6 The monkey lives in the _____.

WORKBOOK
page 56

86

Lesson

1 Listen, read, and say.

GRAMMAR
Where do you live?
I live in the city.

2 Sing and act. **Where Do You Live?**

Where do you live?	Where do you live?	Where do you live?
I live in the desert.	I live in the ocean.	I live in the city.
The desert! The desert!	The ocean! The ocean!	The city! The city!
The sizzling fizzling desert!	The splishy splashy ocean!	The busy whizzy city!

Lesson 7

· FUN READER ·

LET'S VISIT MONGOLIA

1 Read about home life in Mongolia.

Hi! I'm Maa. Welcome to Mongolia! These are my parents.

We don't live in the city. We live in the country. And we don't live in an apartment. We live in a tent! This is our house. It's called a yurt. In Mongolia, a lot of families live in tents. Where do you live?

Think Twice

1 Circle.

In Mongolia, a lot of people live in yurts.   True / False

2 Complete about your country.

houses   boats   trailers
castles   apartments   tents

In _____, a lot of people live in _____. Some people live in _____.

88

Lesson 8

SPEAKING TIME

1 Draw, write, and say.

This is a tent in Mongolia.

This is a / an _____ in my country.

NEW FRIENDS

1 Complete the conversation. Choose your response.

I live in the country. Where do you live?

I live in the _____.

Come and play at my house.

OK. Thank you! ◯   I'd love to. ◯

2 Act out the conversation.

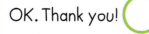

WORKBOOK page 58

89

AUSTRALIA

He's from Australia!

UNIT 8

Lesson 1

·VOCABULARY·

TRACK 67

1 Listen, point, and say.

❶ recorder ❷ trumpet ❸ drums

❹ piano ❺ violin ❻ tambourine

TRACK 68

2 Listen and guess.

3 Act and say.

I like playing the piano!

I like playing the trumpet!

I like playing the violin!

WORKBOOK page 59

92

Lesson 2

TRACK 69

1 Listen, read, and say.

> **GRAMMAR**
> **Do you play** board games?
> Yes, **I do**. / No, **I don't**.

2 Complete and circle.

1 Do you _____ the trumpet? Yes, I do. / No, I don't.
2 _____ play the drums? Yes, I do. / No, I don't.

3 Ask and answer.

> the piano   the recorder   the violin
> soccer   computer games   board games

Do you play the piano?

Yes, I do.

93

Lesson 3

SOUNDS GREAT

1 Listen and chant.

Put on your coat,
Get in the boat,
Sit down low,
And row, row, row!

2 Listen, say, and color.

   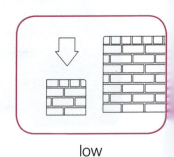

boat　　　　row　　　　coat　　　　low

3 Look and write.

 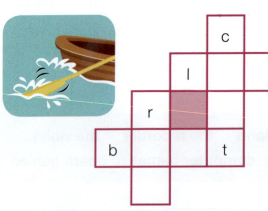 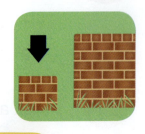 

4 Read the chant and underline *oa* and *ow*.

WORKBOOK
page 61

94

Lesson 4   · READING TIME ·

1 Listen and read.

 2 Read the story again. Check (✓) the **value**.

Play an instrument. ◯   Help your friends. ◯

 3 How do you help your friends? Circle.

I help my friends to **play computer games** / **make models** / **climb trees** / **do homework** / **spell**.

95

Lesson 5

VOCABULARY

TRACK 73

1 Listen, point, and say.

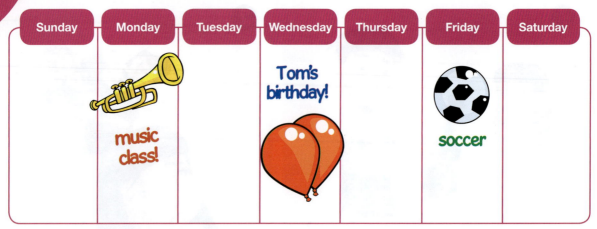

TRACK 74

2 Listen and say what's next.

3 Make a chart and say.

"I play the trumpet on Mondays."

WORKBOOK page 63

Lesson 6

TRACK 75

1 Listen, read, and say.

GRAMMAR
Does he / she play soccer **on** Tuesdays?
Yes, **he / she does.**
No, **he / she doesn't.**

TRACK 76

2 Sing and act. **Action Girl**

Does she play soccer on Mondays?
Does she play the trumpet on Tuesdays?
Yes, she does. Yes, she does.
She's an action girl.

Does she do taekwondo on Wednesdays?
Does she play the piano on Thursdays?
Yes, she does. Yes, she does.
She's an action girl.

Does she go to sleep on Fridays?
Does she go to sleep on Fridays?
Yes, she does. Yes, she does.
She's a very tired girl!

97

Lesson 7

· FUN READER ·

LET'S VISIT AUSTRALIA

1 Read about a boy from Australia.

My name is Bahloo. I'm from Australia.

I like listening to and playing music. I'm a musician. I play the drums, the tambourine, and a special instrument called the didgeridoo. It's a traditional musical instrument from Australia.

After school, I play music on Mondays, Wednesdays, and Fridays. On Tuesdays and Thursdays, I draw pictures. On Saturdays and Sundays, I make models and I paint. I'm very creative!

Think Twice

1 What does Bahloo like doing? Circle.

painting / playing the drums / playing soccer / drawing / watching TV

2 Do you like music and art?

Lesson 8

SPEAKING TIME

 1 Draw, write, and say.

> This is a musician from my country. He / She likes playing the _____.

NEW FRIENDS

1 Complete the conversation. Choose your response.

> I play the drums, the tambourine, and the didgeridoo. Do you play a musical instrument?

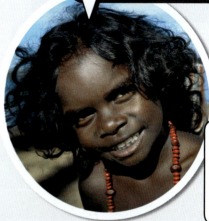

> Yes, I do. I play the _____. ○
>
> No, I don't. ○

2 Act out the conversation.

WORKBOOK
page 65

99

PROGRESS CHECK

✓ 1 Look, match, and write.

1 _____ in a cave.
2 _____ in a trailer.
3 _____ in a boat.
4 _____He lives_____ in a castle.

✓ 2 Look and complete. Then ask and answer.

Where _____ you _____ ?

I _____ in the _____ .

Where _____ ?

I _____ in _____ .

THINK AGAIN!

A typical home in Mongolia is a _____.

My favorite lesson is on page _____.

An animal from Mongolia is _____.

100

WORKBOOK page 66

STICKERS

PASSPORT page 14

PROGRESS CHECK

 1 Write *Yes, I do.* or *No, I don't.*

1 Do you play the piano? _____.
2 Do you play the trumpet? _____.
3 Do you play the tambourine? _____.
4 Do you play the drums? _____.
5 Do you play the violin? _____.
6 Do you play the recorder? _____.

2 Look and write *Yes, he does.* or *No, he doesn't.*

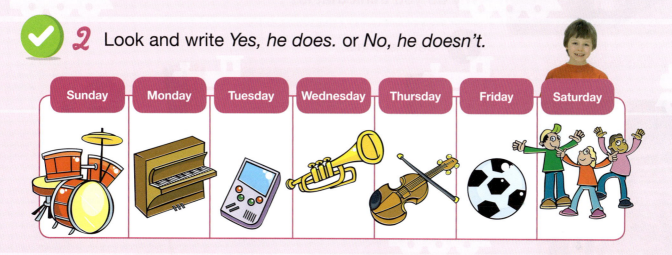

| Sunday | Monday | Tuesday | Wednesday | Thursday | Friday | Saturday |

1 Does he play the piano on Mondays? _____.
2 Does he play soccer on Thursdays? _____.
3 Does he play the trumpet on Fridays? _____.
4 Does he play with friends on Saturdays? _____.
5 Does he play the tambourine on Sundays? _____.

THINK AGAIN!

A traditional instrument from Australia is the _____.

My favorite picture is on page _____.

My favorite lesson is on page _____.

WORKBOOK page 67

STICKERS

PASSPORT page 16

101

MONGOLIA

This is a traditional home in Mongolia called a *ger*.

The wood is painted with patterns.

Neighbors live next to each other.

STEAM

TEAM NAME

Nomadic people move their home from place to place. Why do you think that is?

1 Get materials.

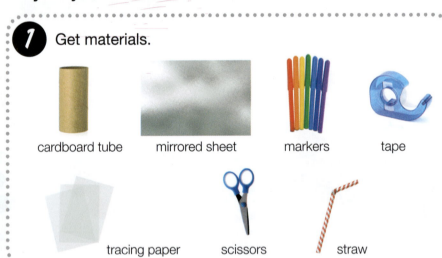

cardboard tube   mirrored sheet   markers   tape

tracing paper   scissors   straw

2 Draw three rectangles on the mirrored sheet. Cut them out.

The patterns on the didgeridoo tell a story.

The patterns on the door are symbols of good wishes.

102

 **CHALLENGE 4**

MAKE A KALEIDOSCOPE

 **AUSTRALIA**

3 Tape and fold into a triangle.
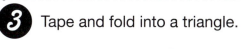

4 Put in tube.

5 Cut straw and tape to top.

6 Decorate tracing paper with a pattern from Mongolia or Australia.
 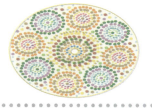

7 Attach pattern to straw. Look into the light!
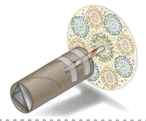

Super Star Challenge
Make a kaleidoscope pattern from a different culture.

Which patterns are traditional in your country?

Aboriginal people paint stories using small circles or dots.

The dot designs fill the painting.

The colors come from nature.

TEAMWORK ★★★★★

103

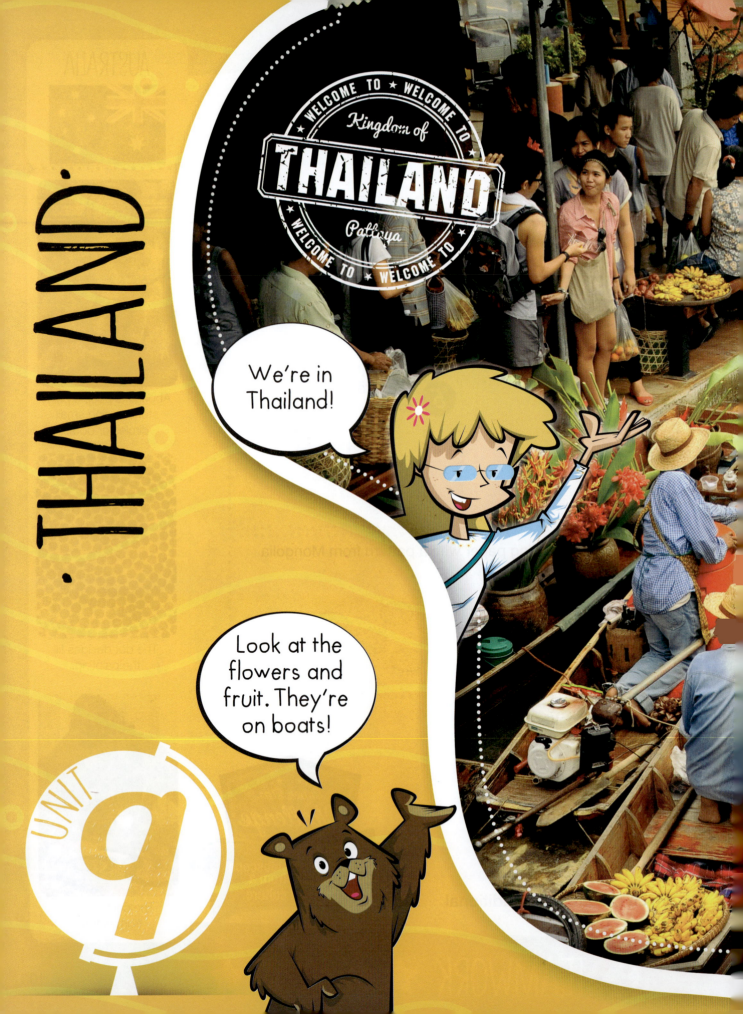

Check (✓) three other types of transportation used in Thailand.

1 2 3 4

 Lesson 1

VOCABULARY

 TRACK 77

1 Listen, point, and say.

1 airplane

2 bus

3 helicopter

4 car

5 train

6 motorcycle

 TRACK 78

2 Listen and guess.

 3 Play the Memory Game.

On my way to school, I see a bus.

On my way to school, I see a bus and a train.

106

WORKBOOK page 68

Lesson 2

TRACK 79

1 Listen, read, and say.

· GRAMMAR ·

I don't go to school **by** train.
I go by bus.
He / She doesn't go to school **by** boat.
He / She goes by train.

2 Complete.

1 He _____ to school by bus.
　He _____ by train.

2 She _____ to school by motorcycle.
　She _____ by bus.

3 Talk to a friend.

> I don't go to school by bus. I go by car.

WORKBOOK
page 69

GRAMMAR GUIDE
page 133

107

Lesson 3

SOUNDS GREAT

1 Listen and chant.

Oh, no! My new blue shoe!
Here! I have some glue for you.

2 Listen, say, and color.

blue

glue

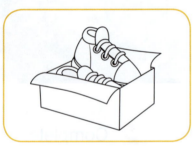

new

3 Write and match.

bl _____ _____   gl _____ _____   n _____ _____

4 Read the chant and underline *ue* and *ew*.

WORKBOOK
page 70

108

Lesson 4 # READING TIME

TRACK 82

1 Listen and read.

2 Read the story again. Check (✓) the **value** ⭐.

Care for the environment.   Walk to the beach.

3 How do you go to the local store? Circle.

WORKBOOK page 71

Lesson 5

VOCABULARY

TRACK 83

1 Listen, point, and say.

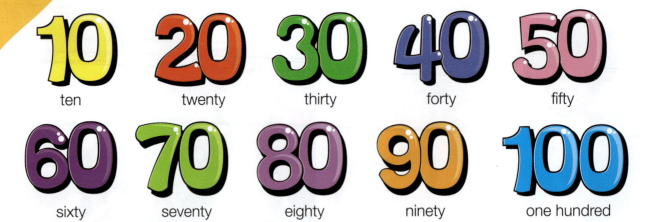

10	20	30	40	50
ten	twenty	thirty	forty	fifty
60	70	80	90	100
sixty	seventy	eighty	ninety	one hundred

2 Match.

100   20   60   10   40   30

forty   twenty   one hundred   thirty   ten   sixty

3 Complete, write, and say.

There are eighty bikes.

WORKBOOK page 72

Lesson 6

> **GRAMMAR**
> **How many** apples **are there**?
> **There are** twenty.

TRACK 84

1 Listen, read, and say.

2 Ask and answer.

pencils   chairs   windows   desks

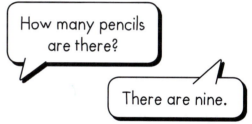

TRACK 85

3 Sing. **The Picnic Box**

How many apples are there in the picnic box?
There are forty and two,
That makes forty-two …

How many sandwiches are there in the picnic box?
There are twenty and six,
That makes twenty-six …

How many cookies are there in the picnic box?
There are thirty and five,
That makes thirty-five …

WORKBOOK page 73   GRAMMAR GUIDE page 133

111

Lesson 7

· FUN READER ·

LET'S VISIT THAILAND

1 Read about city life in Thailand.

My name is Mali. I live in Bangkok. It's a city in Thailand.

There are a lot of cars, buses, trains, motorcycles, and taxis. Bangkok has special taxis.

Look at this one. It's called a tuk-tuk. It's very colorful. It's blue, yellow, and red. I go to school by tuk-tuk.

This is a taxi, too. It's a river taxi. Some people in Bangkok go to work by river taxi. And some people go to the market by river taxi, too. Are there river taxis in your city?

Think Twice

1 Circle.

Mali goes to school by bus / taxi / tuk-tuk / river taxi.

2 Are there different kinds of taxis in your country?

Lesson 8

SPEAKING TIME

 1 Draw, write, and say.

In Thailand, some people go to work by river taxi. In my country, some people go to work by _____.

NEW FRIENDS

1 Complete the conversation. Choose your response.

Hello. I go to school by tuk-tuk. How do you go to school?

I go to school by _____

I walk to school.

2 Act out the conversation.

WORKBOOK page 74

113

Color the clothes to match the photo.

Lesson **1**

VOCABULARY

 TRACK 86

1 Listen, point, and say.

1. shirt
2. shoes
3. pants
4. sweater
5. skirt
6. sneakers

2 Read, color, and say.

They're blue pants.   It's a green sweater.   It's a pink skirt.

3 Find and circle.

o	b	v	g	m	y	u	z	l	p
s	n	e	a	k	e	r	s	i	a
h	f	m	k	t	c	j	h	p	n
o	q	b	i	x	s	k	i	r	t
e	l	p	y	a	c	m	r	o	s
s	w	b	s	w	e	a	t	e	r

116

WORKBOOK
page 75

Lesson 2

GRAMMAR

This is Maria's sweater.
These are Tom's books.

TRACK 87

1 Listen, read, and say.

This is Maria's skirt.

These are Tom's sneakers.

2 Look and write.

1 These are _____ shoes.

2 This is _____ shirt.

3 Find some things and say.

This is Michael's sweater.

These are Alan's books.

WORKBOOK page 76

GRAMMAR GUIDE page 133

117

Lesson 3

SOUNDS GREAT

TRACK 88

1 Listen and chant.

New clothes for your birthday.
From your mother and me.
Let's sing "Happy Birthday."
One, two, three …

TRACK 89

2 Listen, say, and color.

three　　　　　birthday　　　　　mother　　　　　clothes

3 Write **th** or **th**.

mo ___ ___ er　　___ ___ ree　　clo ___ ___ es　　bir ___ ___ day

 4 Read the chant and underline *th*.

118

WORKBOOK
page 77

Lesson 4 ·READING TIME·

1 Listen and read.

2 Read the story again. Check (✓) the value.

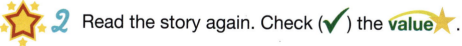

Say "Thank you."   Share with family and friends.

3 What do you share with your family? Circle.

clothes / books / candy / bedroom / toys

UNIT 10

Lesson 5

VOCABULARY

TRACK 91

1 Listen, point, and say.

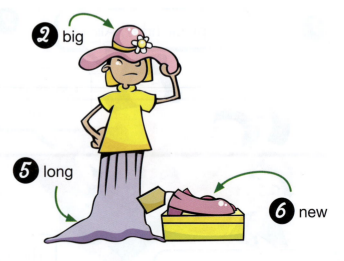

1 small
2 big
3 short
4 old
5 long
6 new

2 Complete.

1 It's a _____ skirt.

4 They're _____ sneakers.

2 It's a _____ shirt.

5 They're _____ pants.

3 They're _____ shoes.

6 They're _____ shoes.

3 Look and talk to a friend.

It's a long skirt.

They're short pants.

WORKBOOK page 79

120

Lesson 6

1 Listen, read, and say.

GRAMMAR
He / She has an old guitar.

2 Complete.

1 Bob _____ hat.

2 Alex _____ dog.

3 Draw, color, and sing. **Our Clothes**

I have a new, new, new shirt.
She has an old, old, old skirt.
He has big, big, big sneakers.
I have small, small, small shoes.
We like our clothes!
We like our clothes!

WORKBOOK page 80

GRAMMAR GUIDE page 133

121

Lesson 7

· FUN READER ·

LET'S VISIT PERU

1 Read about musical instruments from Peru.

I'm Pedro and I'm from Cusco, Peru.

Peru is famous for musical instruments. This is my musical instrument. It's called the pan pipes. The music is very beautiful. The pipes are short and long.

This is my sister. She plays a special guitar from Peru. It's very small, and it's old. My sister likes playing this guitar. She doesn't like playing big guitars. She can play the guitar and the pan pipes.

Think Twice

1 Circle.
   Pedro can play the guitar and the pan pipes.   True / False

2 Do you like music?

122

Lesson 8

SPEAKING TIME

 1 Draw, write, and say.

> This is a special musical instrument from my country. It's called a _____.

NEW FRIENDS

1 Complete the conversation. Choose your response.

Hello. I like playing the pan pipes. Do you like listening to traditional music?

Yes, I do. ◯

Not really. I prefer _____. ◯

2 Act out the conversation.

WORKBOOK page 81

123

PROGRESS CHECK

1 Complete.

    1 _He doesn't go_ to school by motorcycle.
He goes by bike.

    2 _____ to school by bus.
_____ by car.

    3 _____ to school by helicopter.
_____ by train.

   4 _____ to school by airplane.
_____ by taxi.

2 Write. Then ask and answer.

How many butterflies are there?

1 20  + 7 = _27 butterflies_

There are twenty-seven.

2 50 + 2 = _____

3 70 + 1 = _____

4 40 + 7 = _____

THINK AGAIN!

A type of transportation in Thailand is _____.

My favorite lesson is on page _____.

A city in Thailand is _____.

WORKBOOK page 82   **STICKERS**   **PASSPORT** page 18

124

PROGRESS CHECK

 1 Complete and say.

1 Fiona has a _____long skirt_____.

2 Rosy has a _____.

3 Fiona has an _____.

4 Rosy has a _____.

Fiona and Rosy.

 2 Write.

This is _____Fiona's skirt_____.

This is _____.

These are _____.

This is _____.

THINK AGAIN!

A musical instrument from Peru is _____.

My favorite picture is on page _____.

Clothes people wear in Peru are _____.

WORKBOOK page 83   **STICKERS**   **PASSPORT** page 20

125

THAILAND

Paknam temple and Khlong-Dan river, Bangkok.

Amphawa floating market, Bangkok.

The boats in the floating market are small and made of wood.

STEAM

TEAM NAME

Make predictions about objects that will float or sink.

float	sink

1 Select the materials you need to design your boat.

Many Thai boats are decorated with colored ribbons and flowers to pay respect to water spirits.

Some Uru boats have a feline figurehead on the bow. The puma is a sacred animal for the Andean peoples.

CHALLENGE 5

· FLOAT YOUR BOAT ·

PERU

2. Design and build a boat. Look at some examples.

The Uru people live on the islands of Lake Titicaca.

3. Test your boat. Does it sink or float?
_____

4. Add coins to your boat. Does it sink or float?
_____

The islands are made of reeds.

5. Draw your boat.

Super Star Challenge
Work together to design a floating island.

What makes the water a good or a bad place to live?

Balsas are boats made of dried reeds.

TEAMWORK ★★★★☆

127

GRAMMAR GUIDE

HOW TO USE THE GRAMMAR GUIDE

Hello! I'm Grant. I'm your grammar guide. I love grammar! Come and see me after each grammar lesson. I'm here to help you. Follow me!

GRANT'S HOME STUDY GUIDE

1. Read your grammar guide again at home.
2. Look at the example. Close your book. Try to say the example.
3. Open your book and check.

1 After your grammar lessons, turn to the Grammar Guide. Look at the example.

> **Sit down, please.**
> **Don't talk.**

2 Complete the activity.

Complete.

1. Stand ___up___, please.
2. Don't sit _____.
3. Clean up, _____.
4. _____ shout.

3 Check your answers.

Come back and see me if you get lost!

128

 CANADA

 GERMANY

Lesson 2

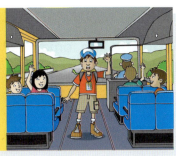

Sit down, please.
Don't run.

Complete.

1 Stand _____, please.
2 Don't sit _____.
3 Clean up, _____.
4 _____ shout.

Lesson 2

What time is it?
It's eight o'clock.

Complete.

1 What _____ is it? It's three _____.
2 _____ _____ is it? _____ two o'clock.
3 What time _____ _____? _____ five _____.

Lesson 6

How do you spell your name?

Complete.

1 How _____ you spell "snake"?
2 _____ do you _____ "panda"?
3 _____ _____ you spell "clock"?
4 _____ do you _____ your name? _____

Lesson 6

I get up at six o'clock.

Complete.

1 I get _____ at _____ o'clock.
2 I have lunch at _____ _____.
3 I _____ dinner at _____ _____ in the evening.
4 I go to bed _____ _____ o'clock at night.

129

 KENYA  TURKEY

Lesson 2

This is a goat.
That's a donkey.
These are chickens.
Those are cows.

Complete.

1 That's _____ chicken.

2 This _____ _____ sheep.

3 Those _____ birds.

4 These _____ ducks.

Lesson 2

Do you like tomatoes?
Yes, **I do**. / No, **I don't**.

Complete.

1 _____ you like onions? Yes, I _____.

2 Do you _____ beans? _____, I do.

3 Do _____ like ants? No, I _____.

4 Do you like _____? _____, I don't.

Lesson 6

What's this / that?   **It's a** ladybug /
                          an ant.

What are these /   **They're**
those?   caterpillars.

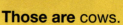

Complete.

1 _____ that?

2 _____ _____ ant.

3 What _____ those?

4 _____ grasshoppers.

Lesson 6

I like pancakes.
I don't like peppers.

Complete.

1 I _____ carrots.

2 I _____ pancakes.

3 I _____ peppers.

4 I _____ cookies.

130

UNIT 5 SOUTH KOREA

UNIT 6 ARGENTINA

Lesson 2

Can you speak Vietnamese?
Yes, **I can**. / No, **I can't**.

Complete.

1 _____ you play the guitar?

   _____, I can.

2 Can _____ jump rope? No, I _____.

3 Can you touch your toes?
   _____.

4 Can you climb a tree?
   _____.

Lesson 6

I / He / She / They can sing.
I / He / She / They can't swim.

Complete.

1 Dogs _____ sing.

2 Birds _____ sing.

3 Dogs _____ fly.

4 Birds _____ fly.

Lesson 2

What do you like doing?
I like play**ing** soccer.
I don't like watch**ing** TV.

Complete.

1 What _____ you like _____?

2 I _____ reading.

3 I _____ like playing soccer.

4 I _____.

Lesson 6

He / She likes paint**ing**.
He / She doesn't like swimm**ing**.

Complete. Write about your friend.

1 He / She likes _____.

2 He / She doesn't like _____.

3 He / She _____.

 # MONGOLIA

 # AUSTRALIA

Lesson 2

He / She / It lives in a house boat.

Write the words in order.

1 She castle lives a in
   _____.

2 trailer a in He lives
   _____.

3 in lives cave It a
   _____.

Lesson 2

Do you play the guitar?
Yes, **I do**. /
No, **I don't**.

Complete.

1 _____ you play the violin? Yes, I _____.

2 Do _____ play the piano? _____, I don't.

3 _____ you _____ soccer? _____, _____ do.

Lesson 6

 Where do you live?
I live in the country.

Complete.

1 _____ do you live?

2 I _____ in the city.

3 Where _____ you _____?

4 I live _____ _____ jungle.

Lesson 6

Does he / she play soccer **on** Tuesdays?
Yes, **he / she does**.
No, **he / she doesn't**.

Complete.

1 _____ he go to the park on Tuesdays? _____, he doesn't.

2 Does _____ play soccer _____ Mondays? Yes, he _____.

3 _____ he _____ to the mall _____ Thursdays? No, _____ _____.

132

 **THAILAND**

 **PERU**

Lesson 2

I don't go to school **by** train.
I go by bus.
He / She doesn't go to school **by** bus.
He / She goes by bike.

Complete.

1. _____ doesn't go to school by train. He _____ by bus.
2. She _____ go to school _____ bike. _____ goes _____ bus.
3. I don't _____.
   I _____.

Lesson 2

This is Maria's backpack.
These are Maria's books.

Complete.

1. This _____ Maria's skirt.
2. _____ are Tom's books.
3. _____ is Alan's shirt.
4. These _____ Grant's sneakers.

Lesson 6

How many pencils **are there**?
There are twenty-four.

Complete.

1. How many apples are _____? _____ are eight.
2. _____ many bananas _____ there? There _____ four.
3. _____ _____ cookies are there? _____ _____ ten.

Lesson 6

He / She has an old guitar.

Write the words in order.

1. He big has hat a
   _____.
2. has short He pants
   _____.
3. new has sneakers He
   _____.

2020 © Macmillan Education do Brasil

Based on *Next Move*
© Macmillan Publishers Limited 2013
Text © Cantabgilly Limited and Mary Charrington 2013
Adapted by Viv Lambert
Grammar Guide written by Viv Lambert
STEAM Challenge sections written by Sarah Elizabeth Sprague
Next Move is a registered trademark, property of Macmillan Publishers, 2013
First edition entitled "Next Stop" published 2009 by Macmillan Publishers

Director of Languages Brazil: Patrícia Souza De Luccia
Publishing Manager and Field Researcher: Patricia Muradas
Content Creation Coordinator: Cristina do Vale
Art Editor: Jean Aranha
Lead Editors: Ana Beatriz da Costa Moreira, Daniela Gonçala da Costa, Luciana Pereira da Silva
Content Editors: Millyane M. Moura Moreira, Tarsílio Soares Moreira
Digital Editor: Ana Paula Girardi
Editorial Assistant: Roberta Somera
Editorial Intern: Bruna Marques
Art Assistant: Denis Araujo
Art Intern: Jacqueline Alves
Graphic Production: Tatiane Romano, Thais Mendes P. Galvão
Proofreaders: Edward Willson, Márcia Leme, Sabrina Cairo Bileski
Design Concept: Design Divertido Artes Gráficas
Page Make-Up: Figurattiva Editorial
Photo Research: Marcia Sato
Image Processing: Jean Aranha, Jacqueline Alves, Denis Araujo
Audio: Argila Music, Núcleo de Criação
Cover Concept: Jean Aranha
Cover photography: TommL/iStockphoto/Getty Images, Bubert/iStockphoto/Getty Images, LokFung/iStockphoto/Getty Images.
Commissioned photography: Macmillan Publishers Ltd/ Paul Bricknell (p. 10, 11, 14, 21, 25, 35, 48, 58, 62, 72, 83, 92, 96, 106, 110, 117, 121).
Map: Allmaps
Illustrations: Adilson Secco (p. 31, 55, 78-79, 102-103), Andrew Painter (p. 7, 11, 15, 17, 18, 21, 25, 35, 39, 45, 49, 53, 59, 63, 69, 73, 83, 87, 93, 97, 100, 107, 111, 117, 121), Anna Godwin (p. 12, 22, 36, 46, 60, 70, 84, 94, 108), Anthony Rule (p.128), David Hurtado (p. 23, 109, 129, 130, 131, 132, 133), Fiona Gowen (p. 37, 118), Harrington Illustration (p. 13, 23, 37, 47, 61, 71, 85, 95, 109, 119), Jim Peacock (p. 15, 20, 21, 28, 29, 53, 58, 63, 72, 73, 76, 77, 96, 100, 101, 110, 120, 124), Rita Giannetti | Sylvie Poggio (p. 20, 34, 35, 48, 49, 52, 53, 82, 97, 111, 124, 125).

Reproduction prohibited. Penal Code Article 184 and Law number 9.610 of February 19, 1998.

We would like to dedicate this book to teachers all over Brazil. We would also like to thank our clients and teachers who have helped us make this book better with their many rich contributions and feedback straight from the classroom!

The authors and publishers would like to thank the following for permission to reproduce the photographic material:
p. 8: CanadaFirst/iStockphoto/Getty Images; p. 10: jaroon/ iStockphoto/Getty Images, sam74100/iStockphoto/ Getty Images, skynesher/iStockphoto/Getty Images, lissart/iStockphoto/Getty Images, szefei/iStockphoto/ Getty Images, Julialine/iStockphoto/Getty Images; p. 16: FamVeld/iStockphoto/Getty Images, Mirceax/ iStockphoto/Getty Images; p. 19: Tim Graham/Getty Images; p. 24: LittleBee80/iStockphoto/Getty Images, Wavebreakmedia/iStockphoto/Getty Images, djedzura/ iStockphoto/Getty Images, SolStock/iStockphoto/ Getty Images, Monkeybusinessimages/iStockphoto/ Getty Images, LittleBee80/iStockphoto/Getty Images, Voyagerix/iStockphoto/Getty Images; p. 26: ferrantraite/ iStockphoto/Getty Images, LauriPatterson/iStockphoto/ Getty Images; p. 30: alexsl/iStockphoto/Getty Images, AK2/iStockphoto/Getty Images, Michel Loiselle, bgrier/ iStockphoto/Getty Images, KeithBinns/iStockphoto/ Getty Images, Professor25/iStockphoto/Getty Images, Nanniie_iiuu/iStockphoto/Getty Images, Andrey_Kuzmin/ iStockphoto/Getty Images, Punkbarby/iStockphoto/Getty Images, Eduard Lysenko/iStockphoto/Getty Images, Michael Burrell/iStockphoto/Getty Images, Tolga TEZCAN/ iStockphoto/Getty Images, Ralf Menache/iStockphoto/ Getty Images; p. 31: 221A/iStockphoto/Getty Images, nedomacki/iStockphoto/Getty Images, Claudio Caridi/ iStockphoto/Getty Images, KenWiedemann/iStockphoto/ Getty Images; p. 32: elmvilla/iStockphoto/Getty Images; p. 33: AWM_Bonke/iStockphoto/Getty Images, wakila/ iStockphoto/Getty Images, Image Source/iStockphoto/ Getty Images, fieldwork/iStockphoto/Getty Images; p. 38: AlexStar/iStockphoto/Getty Images, ithinksky/ iStockphoto/Getty Images, arlindo71/iStockphoto/Getty Images, doug4537/iStockphoto/Getty Images, Liliboas/ iStockphoto/Getty Images, Anest/iStockphoto/Getty Images, luckyraccoon/iStockphoto/Getty Images; p. 40: vlad_karavaev/iStockphoto/Getty Images, Rob Pauley/ iStockphoto/Getty Images, Jonathan Ross/iStockphoto/ Getty Images, brytta/iStockphoto/Getty Images; p. 43: sfe-co2/iStockphoto/Getty Images, flapbocco/ iStockphoto/Getty Images, gofotograf/iStockphoto/Getty Images, sasaperic/iStockphoto/Getty Images, Levent Konuk/iStockphoto/Getty Images; p. 44: Olga Danylenko/ iStockphoto/Getty Images, yay micro/Easypix, Razvan/ iStockphoto/Getty Images, digitalr/iStockphoto/Getty Images, kolesnikovserg/iStockphoto/Getty Images, Ekaterina_Lin/iStockphoto/Getty Images; p. 50: narvikk/ iStockphoto/Getty Images, talip/iStockphoto/Getty Images, tataks/iStockphoto/Getty Images; p. 54: liangpv/ iStockphoto/Getty Images, WLDavies/iStockphoto/Getty Images, Bartosz Hadyniak/iStockphoto/Getty Images, urosr/iStockphoto/Getty Images, Pazhyna/iStockphoto/ Getty Images,Photokanok/iStockphoto/Getty Images, GlobalP/iStockphoto/Getty Images, PhotoEuphoria/ iStockphoto/Getty Images, design56/iStockphoto/Getty Images, Max2611/iStockphoto/Getty Images, JackF/ iStockphoto/Getty Images; p. 55: liangpv/iStockphoto/

Getty Images, graphixel/iStockphoto/Getty Images, florin1961/iStockphoto/Getty Images, Anadolu Agency/Getty Images; p. 56: pius99/iStockphoto/Getty Images; p. 62: marcutti/iStockphoto/Getty Images, hanapon1002/iStockphoto/Getty Images, LumineImages/iStockphoto/Getty Images, PeopleImages/iStockphoto/Getty Images, SerrNovik/iStockphoto/Getty Images, Trout55/iStockphoto/Getty Images; p. 64: Sirikornt/iStockphoto/Getty Images, ma-no/iStockphoto/Getty Images, Alamy/Fotoarena; p. 65: Carl Court/Getty Images; p. 66: holgs/iStockphoto/Getty Images; p. 67: Alamy/Fotoarena, Gerville/iStockphoto/Getty Images, ozgurdonmaz/iStockphoto/Getty Images, Alamy/Fotoarena; p. 68: szirtesi/iStockphoto/Getty Images, AndreyPopov/iStockphoto/Getty Images, Neustockimages/iStockphoto/Getty Images, iofoto/iStockphoto/Getty Images, Wavebreakmedia/iStockphoto/Getty Images, nd3000/iStockphoto/Getty Images, Tolikoff Photography/iStockphoto/Getty Images, DragonImages/iStockphoto/Getty Images, arekmalang/iStockphoto/Getty Images; p. 74: Choreograph/iStockphoto/Getty Images, yacobchuk/iStockphoto/Getty Images; p. 78: liangpv/iStockphoto/Getty Images, Im Yeongsik/iStockphoto/Getty Images, valentinrussanov/iStockphoto/Getty Images, vanbeets/iStockphoto/Getty Images, TwilightShow/iStockphoto/Getty Images, Ziva_K/iStockphoto/Getty Images, deepblue4you/iStockphoto/Getty Images, Eduard Lysenko/iStockphoto/Getty Images, Marco Tulio/iStockphoto/Getty Images, RusN/iStockphoto/Getty Images, Phawintphat/iStockphoto/Getty Images, chromatos/iStockphoto/Getty Images, tttuna/iStockphoto/Getty Images, malerapaso/iStockphoto/Getty Images, svrid79/iStockphoto/Getty Images, pius99/iStockphoto/Getty Images; p. 79: diverroy/iStockphoto/Getty Images, piccaya/iStockphoto/Getty Images, piccaya/iStockphoto/Getty Images, Alamy/Fotoarena; p. 80: Lucy Brown/iStockphoto/Getty Images, Goddard_Photography/iStockphoto/Getty Images, namibelephant/iStockphoto/Getty Images, Windofchange64/iStockphoto/Getty Images, afhunta/iStockphoto/Getty Images; p. 86: DarrenMower/iStockphoto/Getty Images, VSFP/iStockphoto/Getty Images, hectojcm/iStockphoto/Getty Images, LuCaAr/iStockphoto/Getty Images, scaliger/iStockphoto/Getty Images, RuudMorijn/iStockphoto/Getty Images; p. 88: Rawpixel/iStockphoto/Getty Images, Tuul & Bruno Morandi/Getty Images, withgod/iStockphoto/Getty Images; p. 89: molloykeith/iStockphoto/Getty Images; p. 90: Ida Jarosova/iStockphoto/Getty Images; p. 92: Bronwyn8/iStockphoto/Getty Images, istudio5/iStockphoto/Getty Images, ajkkafe/iStockphoto/Getty Images, Wavebreakmedia/iStockphoto/Getty Images, Wavebreakmedia/iStockphoto/Getty Images, Martinan/iStockphoto/Getty Images; p. 98: Lonely Planet Images/Getty Images, Violetastock/iStockphoto/Getty Images, Paul Patton/iStockphoto/Getty Images; p. 102: Panya-/iStockphoto/Getty Images, Bartosz Hadyniak/iStockphoto/Getty Images, bizoo_n/iStockphoto/Getty Images, gionnixxx/iStockphoto/Getty Images, zelg/iStockphoto/Getty Images,UIG/Glow Images, Beto Celli, Lemon_tm/iStockphoto/Getty Images, letoosen/iStockphoto/Getty Images, chromatos/iStockphoto/Getty Images, Coprid/iStockphoto/Getty Images, Michael Burrell/iStockphoto/Getty Images, Eduard Lysenko/iStockphoto/Getty Images, koya79/iStockphoto/Getty Images; p. 103: bodrumsurf/iStockphoto/Getty Images, Photoresearchers/Latinstock, kira_an/iStockphoto/Getty Images, Lonely Planet Images/iStockphoto/Getty Images, kira_an/iStockphoto/Getty

Images; p. 104: nimon_t/iStockphoto/Getty Images; p. 105: tbradford/iStockphoto/Getty Images, Halfpoint/iStockphoto/Getty Images, ayaka_photo/iStockphoto/Getty Images, olaser/iStockphoto/Getty Images; p. 106: Travellinglight/iStockphoto/Getty Images, mladn61/iStockphoto/Getty Images, Balefire9/iStockphoto/Getty Images, Tramino/iStockphoto/Getty Images, sculpies/iStockphoto/Getty Images, Ljupco/iStockphoto/Getty Images; p. 112: pat138241/iStockphoto/Getty Images, intek1/iStockphoto/Getty Images, Leonardo Monteverde/iStockphoto/Getty Images; p. 114: Bartosz Hadyniak/iStockphoto/Getty Images; p. 116: GaryAlvis/iStockphoto/Getty Images, kunchit2512/iStockphoto/Getty Images, popovaphoto/iStockphoto/Getty Images, NYS444/iStockphoto/Getty Images, popovaphoto/iStockphoto/Getty Images, PaulPaladin/iStockphoto/Getty Images; p. 122: hadynyah/iStockphoto/Getty Images, cuklom/iStockphoto/Getty Images, Jose Girarte/iStockphoto/Getty Images; p. 126: liangpv/iStockphoto/Getty Images, NicolasMcComber/iStockphoto/Getty Images, Photoprofi30/iStockphoto/Getty Images, enviromantic/iStockphoto/Getty Images,letty17/iStockphoto/Getty Images,viviamo/iStockphoto/Getty Images, izusek/iStockphoto/Getty Images,RTimages/iStockphoto/Getty Images, vuk8691/iStockphoto/Getty Images, Uwe-Bergwitz/iStockphoto/Getty Images, photka/iStockphoto/Getty Images, imon_t/iStockphoto/Getty Images; p. 127: VanReeel/iStockphoto/Getty Images, hadynyah/iStockphoto/Getty Images, 1001nights/iStockphoto/Getty Images, traveler1116/iStockphoto/Getty Images.

Dados Internacionais de Catalogação na Publicação (CIP)

Bibliotecária responsável: Aline Graziele Benitez CRB-1/3129

C23n Cant, Amanda

1.ed.   Next Station 2: Student's Book / Amanda Cant, Mary Charrington, Sarah Elizabeth Sprague; [Adapt.] Viv Lambert. – 1.ed. – São Paulo: Macmillan Education do Brasil, 2020.

136 p.; il.; 21 x 27 cm. – (Coleção Next Station)

ISBN: 978-85-511-0128-5

1. Língua inglesa. I. Charrington, Mary. II. Sprague, Sarah Elizabeth. III. Lambert, Viv. IV. Título. V. Série.

CDD 420

Índice para catálogo sistemático:

1. Língua inglesa

All rights reserved.

MACMILLAN EDUCATION DO BRASIL
Av. Brigadeiro Faria Lima, 1.309, 3º Andar –
Jd. Paulistano – São Paulo – SP – 01452-002
www.macmillan.com.br
Customer Service: [55] (11) 4613-2278
0800 16 88 77
Fax: [55] (11) 4612-6098

Impresso no Brasil, Eskenazi, 12 2024

· MAP STICKERS ·

· PASSPORT STICKERS ·